AF428123

THE HOLY SEE

A KID'S GUIDE TO EXPLORING THE VATICAN CITY

Geography Book Grade 6
Children's Geography & Culture Books

Speedy Publishing LLC

40 E. Main St. #1156

Newark, DE 19711

www.speedypublishing.com

Copyright 2017

All Rights reserved. No part of this book may be reproduced or used in any way or form or by any means whether electronic or mechanical, this means that you cannot record or photocopy any material ideas or tips that are provided in this book.

In this book, we're going to talk about places to explore in the Vatican City. So, let's get right to it!

Sometimes "The Holy See" and "The Vatican City" are used interchangeably, but they actually have different meanings.

Saint Peter's square in Vatican City

THE VATICAN CITY

The Vatican City is actually a country. In the year 1929, the government of Italy signed a treaty that designated the Vatican City as its own country with its own government. Even though it's officially recognized as a nation, it doesn't vote at the United Nations. Instead, members of the Vatican City act as observers during sessions of the UN.

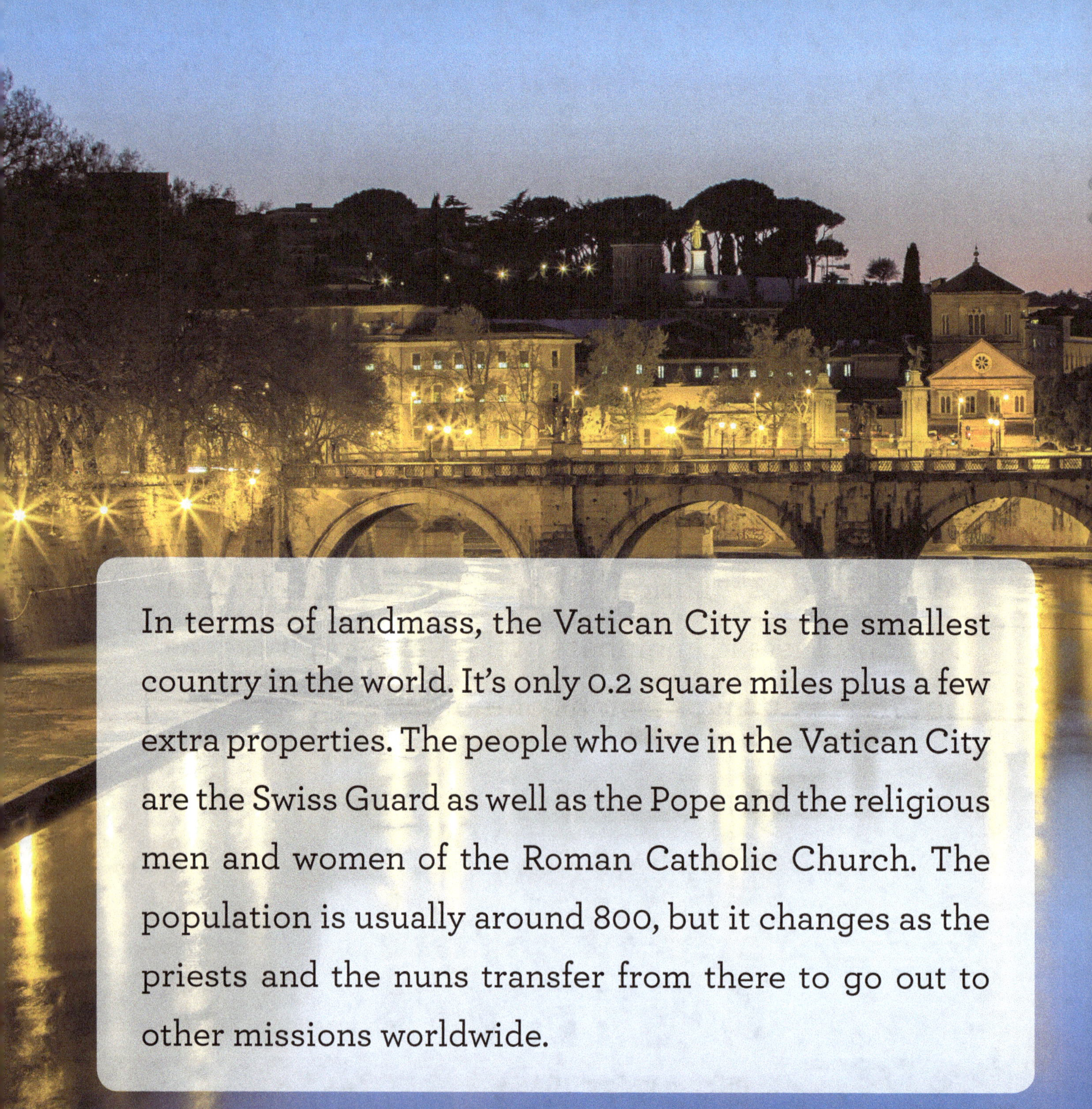

In terms of landmass, the Vatican City is the smallest country in the world. It's only 0.2 square miles plus a few extra properties. The people who live in the Vatican City are the Swiss Guard as well as the Pope and the religious men and women of the Roman Catholic Church. The population is usually around 800, but it changes as the priests and the nuns transfer from there to go out to other missions worldwide.

Vatican City

IN HONOREM PRINCIPIS APOS PAVLVS V BVRGHESIVS ROMANVS PONT MAX AN MDCXII PONT VII

THE HOLY SEE

The Roman Catholic Church refers to itself as the Holy See unless the geographic area of the Vatican City is being discussed. The Holy See means the Holy Chair because "see" comes from the Latin word "sedes," which means "chair."

It signifies St. Peter's chair because Jesus told Saint Peter that he was the "rock" upon which the church would be built. In other words, this meant that Jesus gave Saint Peter the authority to lead all of His followers. The popes who were the leaders of the Roman Catholic Church were given the authority of St. Peter's chair to preside over the 1.1 billion members of the Catholic Church worldwide.

One of many altars in basilica St Peters

View of the Vatican gardens

PLACES TO EXPLORE IN THE VATICAN CITY

Despite the fact that the Vatican City is so small, there are many beautiful and historic places to visit and it would take several days to see everything there is to see.

ST. PETER'S BASILICA

At the center of the Vatican City is the majestic St. Peter's Basilica, a masterpiece of Renaissance architecture. The huge nave, which is the area where the congregation sits, is 185 meters in length and 46 meters in height. From that height, the dome, which was designed by Michelangelo, rises another 119 meters toward the sky.

St Peter's Basilica

Altar and dome in St. Peter's Basilica

The dome is positioned on four huge piers that have a pentagon shape. Below the dome is the bronze canopy of the Pope's altar, which is called the "baldacchino." Made of 100,000 pounds of the precious metal, it was designed by Bernini in the Baroque style. It is considered to be his greatest masterpiece. Beneath the altar is St. Peter's tomb. There are also many other papal tombs within the basilica's walls.

More than 60,000 people can be seated to worship within this massive church, which is the largest Christian church in the world. St. Peter's Basilica was originally built in 326 AD close to the site where St. Peter was martyred. The current structure was built over a long period of time beginning in the 16th century and ending in the 18th century.

ONOREM PRINCIPIS APOST PAVLVS V BVRGHESIVS ROMANVS PONT MAX AN MDC XII PONT VII

IN HONOREM PRINCIPIS APOST PAVLVS V BVRGHESIVS ROMANVS PONT MAX AN MDCXII PONT VII

The basilica is filled with masterpieces as soon as you enter. You go through the double bronze doors, which were salvaged from the original structure. In the portico, there is a statue by Bernini of Emperor Constantine who was the first Christian emperor of Rome. The sculpture shows the emperor gazing toward heaven as he travels on a galloping horse.

As you walk through the church, you will see what appear to be paintings or frescoes on the walls, but your eyes will have deceived you. These "paintings" are actually mosaics that were created with small fragments of glass called "tesserae."

Interior of the St. Peter Basilica

Another very famous masterpiece housed there is Michelangelo's Pietà, which he sculpted when he was only 25 years old. This beautiful statue carved from Carrara marble shows the Virgin Mary as she grieves over Christ's crucified body. In 1972, a mentally ill man tried to destroy this centuries-old masterpiece, so it's now shielded behind bulletproof glass.

From inside the dome, you can make the steep climb up 330 steps to reach the lantern. At the top, you can observe the dome's structure and see an incredible view of St. Peter's Square.

Sistine Chapel

THE SISTINE CHAPEL

The Pope uses the Sistine Chapel to celebrate mass and for other special events. When a pope dies, the cardinals of the Church assemble there to select a new pope, so it is an important building. The building of the chapel was commissioned by Pope Sixtus IV between 1473 to 1484.

The chapel's left and right walls were painted for Sixtus by some of the most famous painters during his papacy, such as Perugino and Botticelli. As you enter the chapel, the left side has paintings that depict the Old Testament and to the right are scenes from the New Testament. These paintings reflect the beginnings of the philosophy of humanism, which recognized that human beings were important to the major events in history.

The dome of the Sistine Chapel

The Sistine Chapel

In 1508, Pope Julius II commissioned Michelangelo to paint the ceiling of the chapel, which at that time was painted blue with stars. Michelangelo was working on statues for the Pope's tomb at the time, and since he considered himself to be a sculptor, not a painter, he wasn't pleased with this assignment.

Originally, he was supposed to be painting the twelve apostles, but instead Michelangelo proposed an ambitious plan to show scenes from the Old Testament's description of the Creation. These depictions were from the Book of Genesis beginning with God separating light from darkness and creating the sun and the moon. One of the most famous paintings shows God reaching out with His finger to touch Adam's finger and give him life.

The Sistine Chapel

The Sistine Chapel

Over twenty years later, Michelangelo was commissioned to paint The Last Judgment for the altar wall. It shows a dynamic image of Jesus as He separates those who will enter heaven from those who will enter hell. Michelangelo's paintings in the Sistine Chapel are dramatic masterpieces of the Renaissance era.

For fourteen years, beginning in 1980, Michelangelo's masterpieces were restored with care. Centuries of soot, varnish, and overpainting were stripped away, revealing his work with its original vibrant colors.

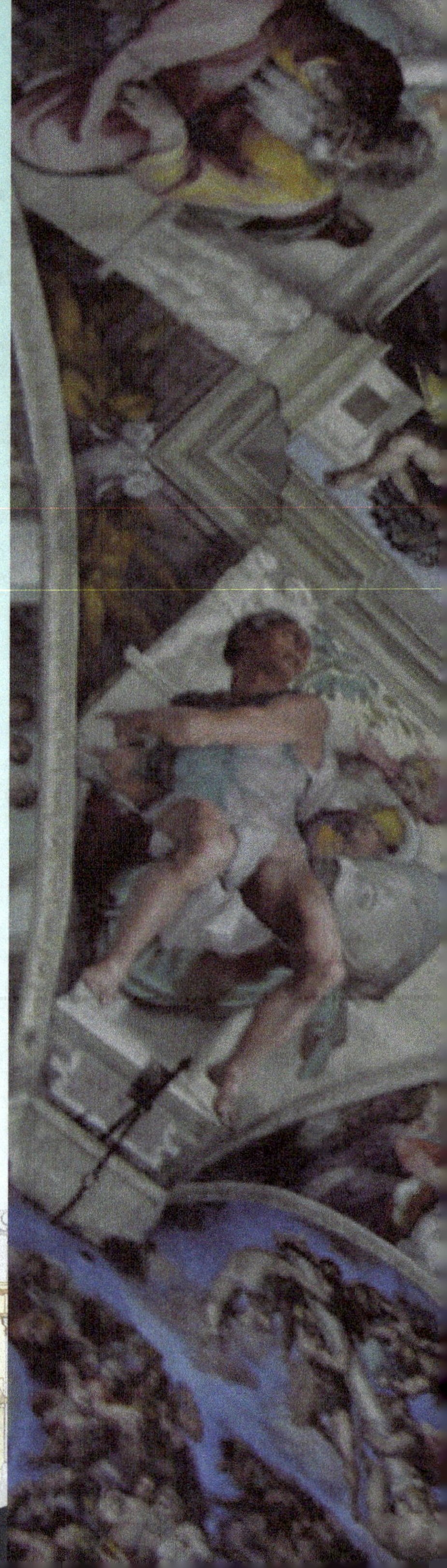

Sistine Chapel paintings

The Pinacoteca of the Vatican

THE PINACOTECA

The Pinacoteca, which means "picture gallery," has 16 rooms filled with masterpieces dating from the Middle Ages to modern works. It's considered to be the best gallery of paintings in all of Rome. Because the works are arranged chronologically, the gallery provides the viewer with a history of how Western painting developed throughout the ages.

One of the most famous paintings from the many works by master artists is the beautiful painting The Transfiguration. This painting was not quite finished when it was found in Raphael's studio when he died at the young age of 37.

The Transfiguration

The Pinacoteca, Vatican City

Other major masterpieces displayed in the Pinacoteca are:

- Stefaneschi Triptych, which is a three-paneled altar piece painted by Giotto in 1320
- Madonna and Child with Saints, painted by Perugino in 1496
- St. Jerome, painted by Leonardo da Vinci in 1482, but left unfinished
- Deposition from the Cross, painted by Caravaggio in 1604

THE RAPHAEL ROOMS

In the Palace of the Vatican there is a suite of four rooms that are used as a reception area, which is the public section of the Pope's apartments. These rooms are famous for the beautiful frescoes that were painted by the painter Raphael and his students.

The School of Athens

The second room of the suite, called the "Stanza della Segnatura" is thought to be the highlight and was painted between 1508 and 1511. In this room, Raphael created the fresco called The School of Athens, which shows a gathering of famous philosophers throughout the ages. He painted his own face into the painting as well as some of the faces of fellow artists of the Renaissance including Leonardo da Vinci.

THE VATICAN LIBRARY

Founded in 1450 AD, the Vatican Library is the richest library worldwide. It contains 7,000 incunabula, which are books that were printed before 1501 AD. It also houses over 25,000 medieval books that were written by hand.

Vatican Library

View of the Vatican Library in the eighteenth century

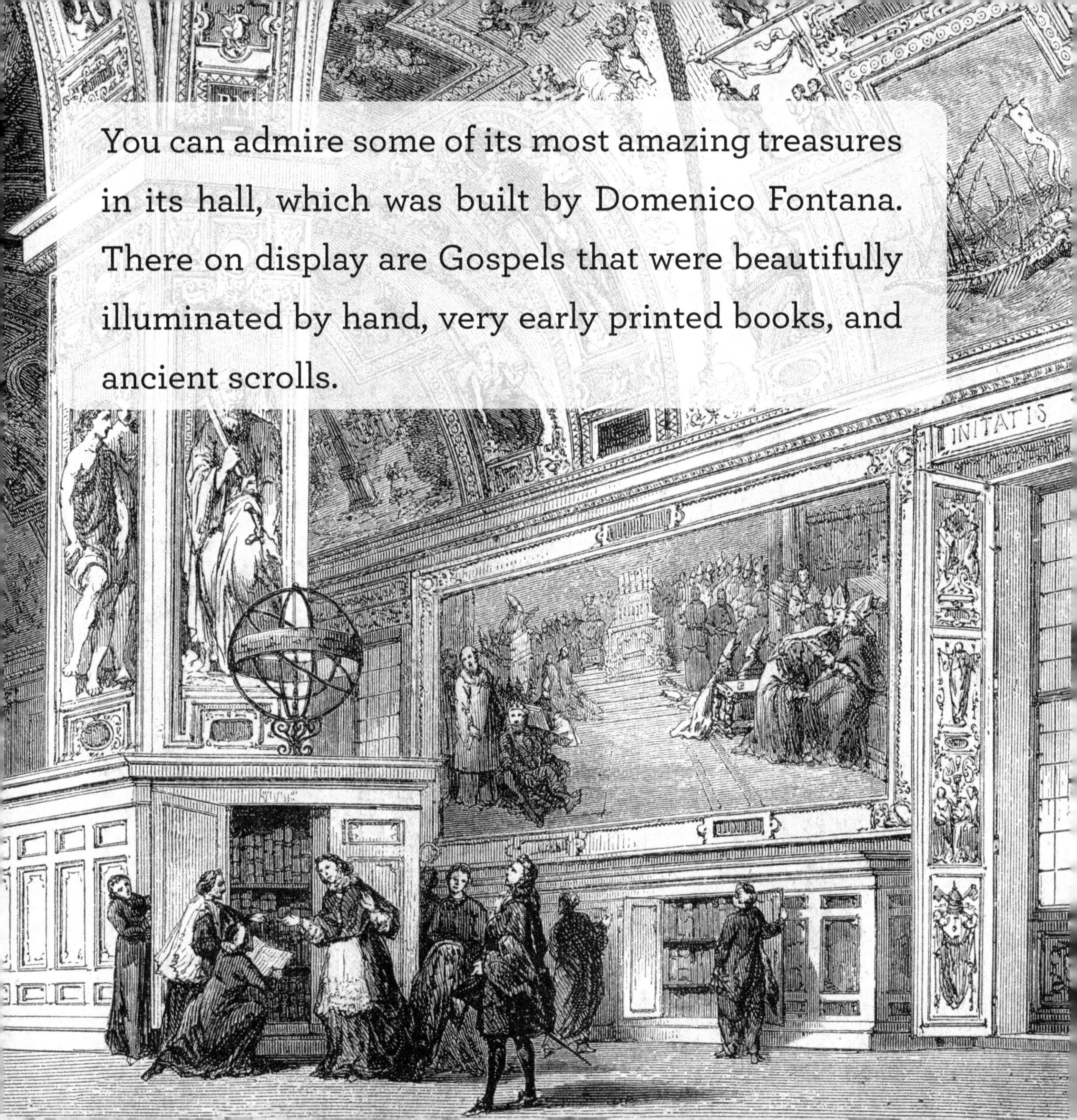

You can admire some of its most amazing treasures in its hall, which was built by Domenico Fontana. There on display are Gospels that were beautifully illuminated by hand, very early printed books, and ancient scrolls.

SUMMARY

Although the Vatican City is the smallest nation in the world and covers a landmass of only 0.2 square miles, it is the center of the governing body of the Roman Catholic Church called the Holy See. It also contains some of the most beautiful architecture and art masterpieces that the world has ever known.

NCIPIS A POST PAVLVS V BVRG SIVS ROMANVS PONT MAX AN

LVS·V·BVRGHESIVS·ROMANVS·ONT·MAX·AN·MD·

Many priceless sculptures and paintings are housed in Saint Peter's Basilica, the Sistine Chapel, the Pinacoteca, and the Raphael Rooms. The Vatican Library houses amazing literary treasures, such as hand-illuminated volumes from the Middle Ages.

Awesome! Now that you know more about the Vatican City, you may want to find out more about the history of Ancient Rome in the Baby Professor book The Ancient City of Rome.

MANVS PONT MAX AN MDCXII PONT V

Visit
BABY PROFESSOR
EDUCATION KIDS
www.BabyProfessorBooks.com
to download Free Baby Professor eBooks
and view our catalog of new and exciting
Children's Books

www.ingramcontent.com/pod-product-compliance
Lightning Source LLC
Chambersburg PA
CBHW060226120726
48009CB00003B/169